Reaching Higher

CHARLES C. WALCUTT
GLENN McCRACKEN

Consultants:
HELENE C. BROOME
GWEN FULWILER
MARETA H. VARNER

Lippincott Basic Reading C

HARPER & ROW, Publishers New York   Philadelphia   Hagerstown   San Francisco   London

1817

Acknowledgments

Grateful acknowledgment is made to the following authors and publishers to use copyright materials. Every effort has been made to obtain permission to use previously published material. Any errors or omissions are unintentional and the publisher will be grateful to learn of them.

"Fuzzy wuzzy, creepy crawly" by Lillian Schultz Vanada. From SUNG UNDER THE SILVER UMBRELLA. Reprinted by permission of the Association for Childhood Education International, 3615 Wisconsin Avenue, N.W., Washington, D.C. Copyright © 1935 by the Association.

"All the Lassies" adapted from ALL THE LASSIES by Liesel Moak Skorpen. Reprinted by permission of THE DIAL PRESS.

"Bird Nesting Ball" from BEGINNING CRAFTS FOR BEGINNING READERS by Alice Gilbreath, copyright © 1972. Used by permission of Follett Publishing Company, a division of Follett Corporation.

"Kite" from MORE BEGINNING CRAFTS FOR BEGINNING READERS by Alice Gilbreath, copyright © 1976. Used by permission of Follett Publishing Company, a division of Follett Corporation.

"Little Wind" by Kate Greenaway from UNDER THE WINDOW. Reproduced by permission of Frederick Warne & Company.

"The Oogle Google Goblin" from "The Bath Goblin" in GO TO BED BOOK by Ella Monckton, adapted by permission of Frederick Warne (Publisher), Ltd.

"The Three Billy Goats" adapted from "The Three Goats" from THROUGH THE FARM-YARD GATE by Emilie Poulsson. Reprinted by permission of Lothrop, Lee & Shepard (A Division of William Morrow & Company).

"Park Play" by James S. Tippitt from MY BOOK HOUSE, Vol. 1, edited by Olive Beaupré Miller. Reprinted by permission of Mrs. M. K. Tippitt.

Text of "Going Down the Street" from IN ONE DOOR AND OUT THE OTHER by Aileen Fisher. Copyright © 1969 by Aileen Fisher. By permission of Thomas Y. Crowell, Publishers.

Photo Credits

Cover photo: Dr. E. R. Degginger; p.21: (left) E. Robinson/Tom Stack & Associates, (right) Jacana/Image Bank; p.22: William Curtsinger/*Wake of the Whale,* published by Friends of the Earth and Elsevier-Dutton; pp. 118–122: Roy Morsch.

Art Credits

Ellen Appleby: pp. 13, 14, 99–103, 114–117; Howard Berelson: p. 98; Jan Brett: pp. 25, 26; Dinoff: p. 86; Len Ebert: pp. 7–10, 67–70, 80, 81, 83; Kathleen Garry-McCord: pp. 74–78; Ethel Gold: pp. 16–19, 28, 29, 45, 47, 48, 66, 105; Kathy Hendrickson: pp. 33, 50; Lucinda McQueen: pp. 1–5, 60–62, 64; Sal Murdocca: pp. 6, 11, 12, 15, 20, 24, 27, 30–32, 35, 36, 44, 49, 51, 57, 59, 65, 71, 72, 79, 84, 88, 96, 104, 106, 112; Steven Schindler: pp. 73, 97; Joel Snyder: pp. 23, 52–56, 85, 89, 90, 92–95, 107–111; Lynn Uhde: pp. 40–43; Jennie Williams: pp. 37–39, 58.

CONTENTS

Developmental pages: sh—page 6; Compound words—page 11; ch, tch—page 12; th—page 15; wh—page 20; qu—page 24; xX—page 27; yY—page 30; zZ—page 31; ng—page 32; -ing—page 34; -ed—page 44; -er—page 49; ir, or, ur, ar—page 51; -ay, -y—page 57; -y, -ly, -ey—page 59; soft c—page 65; soft g—page 71; -dge—page 72; -sion, -tion—page 79; short oo—page 84; long oo—page 88; /ō/ow—page 96; ou—page 104; ou—page 106; u, u__e—page 112; ue, ui—page 113.

A Fine Trick

In a big, green forest was a wild plum tree. A little pig and her sister saw the plums.

"The plums are ripe. But we cannot get up the tree," said the little pigs.

In the deep, dark forest was a tiger. The tiger jumped onto the trail. The tiger stopped just behind the little pigs.

1

"I hope I did not scare you," said the bold tiger.

"Not at all," said the little pigs. "Will you please pick some wild plums for us?"

The tiger smiled.

"I like to eat plums," he said. "I will get plums for all of us." The tiger went up the tree.

"A fine meal I will have," he said to himself. "The fat, little pigs will eat the plums and be even fatter."

2

"We can trick the tiger," said the
first little pig.

"How?" asked her sister.

"Wait and see," said the first pig.
"The tiger will get the wild plums.
But the plums will not be for him
to eat."

"Tiger," called the first little
pig. "We can jump up and down.
Can a tiger?"

The tiger tried to jump up and
down and eat plums at the same
time. His paws slipped and he
almost fell.

"Hold on," cried the little pigs.

The pigs jumped up and down on
the trail. The tiger jumped in the
tree. Down came the wild plums
. . . plop, plop, plop onto the trail.

The pigs picked up the plums and
ran. The little pigs ran fast down
the forest trail.

"It was a fine trick," said the
little pig to her sister. "Now we
have lots of plums to eat."

The tiger did not see the plums
fall. He did not see the pigs run
down the trail. The tiger in the tree
just went up and down, up and
down, up and down.

sh

she	shed	shell	shelf
sheep	sheet	shade	shake
shape	share	ship	shop
shirt	short	shore	shine
fish	dish	wish	wash
dash	trash	rush	brush
flash	splash	fresh	finish

The Perfect Present

"Wake up, Shawn," Mom called as she tugged on the sheets.

Shawn was up in a flash. He dressed in shorts and a T-shirt. Shawn will visit his grandpa. His grandpa lives at the seashore.

Shawn waited on the steps for Grandpa. At last he saw Grandpa's car. He dashed off to greet him.

"Are you all set to go?" asked Grandpa.

"Let's go," said Shawn. Mom and Dad waved as Grandpa drove off.

Shawn liked the seashore. He liked to splash in the warm water. Shawn saw little silver fish in the water. He picked up a seashell. "I want Grandpa to see it," he said.

Shawn ran over to Grandpa and handed him the shell. Grandpa smiled and put the shell to his ear.

"I can hear the sea," said Grandpa. He handed the shell back to Shawn.

"I can hear the sea too," cried Shawn.

"Let's get a bite to eat," said
Grandpa. "After we eat, we can
visit some of the shops."

"And I can get a present for
Mom," Shawn said. Shawn dropped
the shell in the sand. He and
Grandpa went to eat and to visit
the shops.

The first shop sold ships in bottles.

"No," said Shawn, "little ships in
bottles are not for Mom."

Grandpa and Shawn went into a
T-shirt shop. The shop had all kinds
of T-shirts.

"No, not for Mom," said Shawn.

Shawn and Grandpa went into lots of shops. But still, Shawn did not find a present for Mom.

The last shop sold seashells. Grandpa and Shawn had the same idea at the same time. Grandpa winked at Shawn.

"I hope I can find it," said Shawn. He ran back to the seat in the shade. The shell was still in the sand! Shawn picked up the shell and waved to Grandpa.

"Now Mom can hear the sea, too," said Shawn. "It is the **perfect** present!"

Compound Words

cupcake	drainpipe	weekend
sunshine	rainstorm	horseback
popcorn	pancake	milkshake
overcoat	seashell	seashore
mealtime	grandma	grandpa
himself	herself	blindfold
grasshopper	handlebars	baseball

ch

chin	check	chest	cheek
cheese	chase	chair	chirp
such	much	rich	lunch
each	reach	beach	branch
bench	porch	bunch	crunch

–tch

catch	match	patch	scratch
watch	pitch	ditch	switch

Chin Chin

Chin Chin sits on a short old bench
And eats from a dish of cheese.
He eats so much and gets so full
He cannot sit at ease.

"I must not fall from the bench,"
    cries Chin,
"Or the cat will catch me, I fear,
And eat me for lunch as I ate the
    cheese.
He is such a bad cat, I hear."

But Chin Chin goes to sleep at last,
And he falls from the bench on his
  chest.
And the cat eats Chin Chin in two
  big bites,
And sits down on the porch to rest.

Chin was a pig to eat so much
And fall asleep as he did.
It made him too full to be awake,
So off the bench he slid.

th

the	then	them	these
those	than	that	this
thin	think	thank	thick
third	three	throat	thunder
with	bath	fifth	month
teeth	north	moth	cloth
other	brother	father	mother
farther	rather	another	together

Cho's Visit to the Dentist

Cho did not eat much of her lunch. She felt as if all her teeth were in pain. Cho's father said, "I think it's time for a visit to the dentist."

Cho and her father had to catch a bus. It seemed like forever before the bus stopped at Third Street.

"Hello, Mr. Kato," said Dr. North. "How are you, Cho?"

Cho just held her cheek.

"Come and sit in the chair," said Dr. North. "We will find the problem and get rid of the pain. Open wide."

Cho tried hard to make a big **O.**

"I see small holes in three teeth," said Dr. North. "I will fill them and that will stop the pain." Cho was glad to hear that.

The dentist filled all the holes in Cho's teeth with silver metal. Now Cho was able to smile again. She started to get up from the chair.

"Wait, Cho," said Dr. North. "I have a little more I want to do." He cleaned all her teeth. Then he gave Cho a brush and asked her to pretend to brush her teeth. Cho brushed across her front teeth.

"That is OK," said Dr. North. "But I also want you to brush up and down. That cleans between the teeth. Here, let me do it." The dentist brushed up and down, then across. Then he gave Cho the brush to keep.

Dr. North asked Cho to come back in three months for a checkup.

Cho and her father thanked Dr. North and started down the hall.

"Dad, can we stop for a snack?" asked Cho.

"Yes, we can," replied her father.

"I'll have a thick milkshake," Cho said to herself. "And I'll have an apple tart or two."

"Cho," called the dentist, "I almost forgot to remind you . . . WATCH THOSE SWEETS!"

"Forget the snack, Dad," said Cho as she waved to Dr. North.

wh

what	when	where	which
white	while	whale	wheat
whenever	whether	whisper	whisker
whip	wheel	whirl	whine
whipped	wheeled	whirled	whined

Whale Tales

A whale is an animal which lives in the sea. But a whale is not a fish.

Whales can bark, moan, scream, and whine. This is how they speak to each other.

When a whale is born, its mother takes care of it for almost twelve months. She keeps it close to her and protects it.

The mother whale feeds the little whale a lot of milk. A little whale

can drink as much milk as in 400
tall glasses.

A whale sheds tears. These tears
help to clean the whale's eyes. The
tears also protect its eyes from salt
in the sea water.

Whales are the biggest animals that
have ever lived. They can get as
big as 100 feet (30 meters). That is
bigger than two buses.

qu

quit	quill	quilt	quilted
quick	quack	quart	quarter
quarrel	quake	quail	queen
queer	quite	quiet	quaint
squirt	squint	square	squash

So Quiet

The queen tossed and rolled on her bed. She pulled the quilt over her ears. The queen had not slept much all winter. She was quite upset and tired.

"Warm milk did not make me sleep," said the queen. "I tried hot baths. That did not help. What can I do? I must get to sleep." But still the queen did not sleep.

At dawn she got up and went to the garden. The air felt warmer. She saw that the trees had begun to get green again.

25

The queen saw ducks on the pond. They had gone to find a warmer home for the winter. Now they were back again.

The ducks began to quack when they saw the queen. All of a sudden the queen began to smile.

Then up the steps she marched. She jumped into her bed and pulled the quilt up under her chin.

"I did not sleep when it was so quiet," said the queen. "But now I can sleep. The quack of the ducks will help me."

The queen rolled over. As quick as a wink, she was fast asleep.

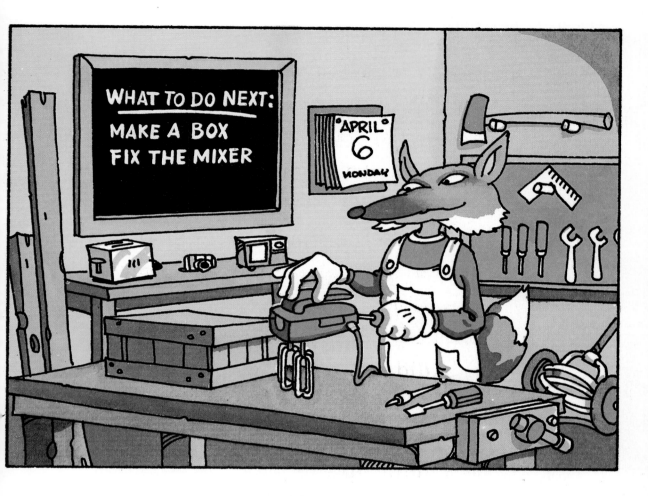

xX

ax	tax	fox	fix
text	next	extra	explore
explain	exit	exact	relax
wax	mix	six	box
waxed	mixer	sixteen	boxes

After All, I'm Six Now

"Exact fare, please," said the bus driver. Roxanne dropped two quarters in the fare box. This was the first time she had been on a bus alone. Her mother had told her to ask the driver to let her off at Fox Street.

But Roxanne said to herself, "I can tell when I get to Grandma's street. There is an old, vacant store on the corner. After all, I'm six now and I can find the street."

At each stop, Roxanne watched for the old, vacant store.

"Next stop—end of the line," said the bus driver. Roxanne was scared.

"I missed the stop," she explained to the driver. "I wanted to get off at Fox Street."

"I have to take the bus back to town again," he said. "I'll let you off at Fox Street."

Roxanne was glad to see her grandmother. Roxanne asked her what had happened to that old store on the corner.

"It was torn down one month ago," she said. "I'm pleased you came to see me. I think you are such a big girl to ride the bus all alone."

"Well, Grandma," said Roxanne, "after all, I'm six now."

yY

yes	yet	yell	yelled
year	yarn	yawn	yank
yoke	yoyo	yard	yardstick

It Begins With Y

When we were on
the lawn, I began
to ___.

Dad had to darn
the socks made
of ___.

Jo lost a card when
she was in the ___.

I can hear the bell.
Do not ___.

Have no fear, we'll
win next ___.

Jill has a net, but
has no fish ___.

zZ

zip	zipper	zebra	zero
zone	zigzag	fizz	whiz
quiz	fuzz	buzz	size
graze	amaze	freeze	breeze
sneeze	squeeze	puzzle	muzzle

An E-Z Quiz

Ten is one and a ___. Bees can ___.

A black and white animal is a ___. Pepper makes me ___.

A soft wind is a ___.

The clerk will ask, "What ___, please?" Water will ___.

–ng

ring	rang	rung	among
sing	sang	song	long
bang	fang	gang	hang
king	wing	bring	thing
spring	string	sting	stung
swing	cling	clung	lung
along	strong	hanger	singer

A Song of Spring

Spring is a time when all is fresh
And birds sing songs in the trees.
Spring is a time when roses bud
And bring sweet smells in the
    breeze.

Spring is a time when the leaves
    are green
And the grass gets long and thick.
It is just the time to string up a
    kite
And go to fish in the creek.

Spring is a time when cowbells
    ring,
Ding-dong. Ding-dong. Ding-dong.
The tree frogs sing so strong and
    clear
And the bees buzz a little song.

–ing

jump	plant	think	yell
jumping	planting	thinking	yelling
singing	catching	fishing	quacking
float	peek	scream	sail
floating	peeking	screaming	sailing
coasting	feeling	reaching	reading

1. Let's go fishing.
2. What are you reading?
3. The boat was floating on the pond.
4. The kids were yelling and screaming.
5. Tell me what you are thinking.
6. How are you feeling now?
7. We went coasting down the hill.
8. All the ducks were quacking.

| sled | whiz | win | shop |
| sledding | whizzing | winning | shopping |

hugging	tugging	running	swimming
hitting	hopping	sitting	stopping
digging	petting	grinning	wagging

1. Mom is sitting on the porch.
2. Let's go swimming in the lake.
3. Grandpa is digging in the garden.
4. Joe is petting his dog.
5. Are the Jets winning the game?
6. I like hugging mom and dad.
7. I saw a frog hopping across the yard.
8. We went shopping for a gift.

hope	drive	chase	smile
hoping	driving	chasing	smiling

making	shaking	skating	waving
shining	poking	diving	saving
hiding	riding	joking	voting

1. Is Anna hiding behind that tree?
2. I am making a sandwich for lunch.
3. Have you ever been to a skating rink?
4. His mom is driving us to class.
5. I keep hoping that we will win.
6. Her dog likes chasing cats.
7. Bob starts shaking when he gets cold.
8. Riding horses is fun.

The Big Hill

Bill and Joan liked to go sledding. They liked to coast down the small hills. But there was one big hill they had never coasted down.

"Let's go coasting down the big hill," said Bill. "Do you think we can do it?"

"Yes," said Joan. "Let's go."

Joan and Bill held on to the sled. The little sled went whizzing down the big hill. It went so fast, Joan felt she was floating in the air. She started yelling at Bill, "Stop! Stop the sled! We are going to crash!"

"I can't stop the sled!" Bill yelled back. "It's going too fast!"

All of a sudden, the sled hit a bump. Joan and Bill both went sailing up in the air. They landed in the soft snow.

Joan called, "Bill, Bill, where are you?" Not far from her the snow started to wiggle.

"Here I am," said Bill, peeking from under a pile of snow.

"I think the small hills are more fun after all," said Bill. "I'll beat you to the top."

Strings and Things

Here are two things you can have fun making from string. Can you think of other things that are fun to do with string?

Bird Nesting Ball

To make a bird nesting ball, you will need:

- a plastic net bag that things come in at the market.
- a cord as long as your arm.
- twisters or yarn to close the bag.
- scraps of cloth, yarn, string, and cotton balls.

Now, starting with step 1—

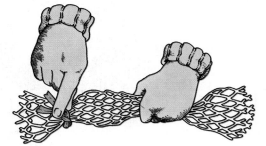

1. Close one end of the bag with yarn or a twister.

2. Put scraps of cloth, yarn, string and the cotton balls inside the bag.

3. Close the other end of the net bag with yarn or a twister.

4. Attach the cord to the nesting ball. Tie the ends of the cord together for hanging.

5. Now the nesting ball is finished. Hang it on a tree branch. In the spring, birds will come to get the soft scraps to make nests. The birds will thank you with a song!

Kite

To make a kite, you
will need:

- a small plastic bag.
- three strings.

Now, starting with step 1—

1. Fold the open end of
   the bag. Make the
   fold as long as your
   fingers. With your
   fingers, pinch along
   the fold.

2. With the  ,
   cut three small slits
   in the folded part of
   the bag.

3. Put a string in each of the holes. Tie each string near the fold.

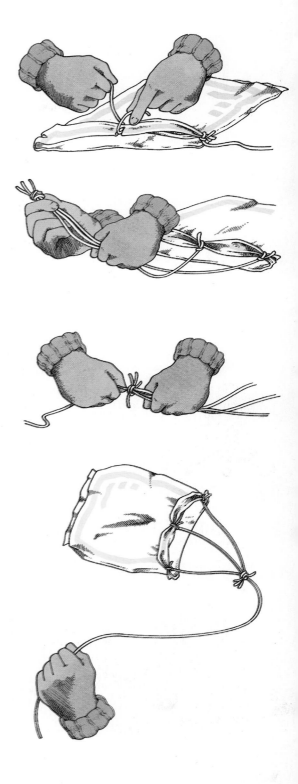

4. Hold the ends of the three strings and tie them together.

5. If you like, you can tie the end of your kite to a longer string.

6. Your kite is finished. Holding the end of your kite, run in a strong wind. The wind will fill your kite with air and make it go UP!

–ed

handed	landed	planted	rested
coasted	weeded	needed	floated
sawed	hammered	cheered	yelled
crossed	helped	reached	finished
stop	trip	dot	plan
stopped	tripped	dotted	planned
wave	smile	care	stare
waved	smiled	cared	stared
joke	choke	shape	hike
joked	choked	shaped	hiked

44

Street of Flowers

One morning, Zelda was sitting on her porch. She wondered what was going on across the street. She wondered what Mr. and Mrs. Kaminski were doing over there.

"Hi!" yelled Zelda.

"Come on over," Mrs. Kaminski called. "I want you to see what we have."

Zelda smiled and crossed the street.

45

"This porch needed cheering up," said Mrs. Kaminski. "So Mr. Kaminski sawed and hammered and made this flower box for me. I'm going to fill the box with flowers and put it on the porch railing."

"Do you mind if I help?" asked Zelda.

"Not at all," said Mrs. Kaminski. "Help is just what we need."

Zelda helped her fill the flower box with dirt. Then they planted the flowers in the box. Zelda picked up the watering can and sprinkled water on the flowers.

"I wish I had a flower box," said Zelda.

"Do you want to make one?" asked Mr. Kaminski. "I still have some lumber left in the basement."

"That will be fun," said Zelda.

Mrs. Kaminski gave Zelda some
small pink flowers to plant in the
box when it was finished.

Zelda's mom and dad were pleased
when they saw the flower box on
the railing. Zelda's mother smiled
and said, "I just love these flowers,
Zelda. The porch needed cheering
up. I wish the rest of the block had
flowers like these."

"I have an idea!" said Zelda.
"Let's ask people in the block to
come and see the flowers."

Zelda and her mom and dad
stopped at one home after the other.
"Please come and see the flowers
we planted," they said.

The next week, other people
began hammering and sawing,
digging and planting. They smiled,
joked, and helped each other. The
flowers cheered up the block **and**
the people. Now Zelda's block was
like one big flower garden.

−er

other	mother	brother	sister
fever	hanger	whisker	shower
long	short	thick	quick
longer	shorter	thicker	quicker
singer	gardener	pitcher	catcher
bake	drive	skate	hike
baker	driver	skater	hiker
miner	rider	smoker	washer
swim	shop	drum	run
swimmer	shopper	drummer	runner
thinner	winner	hotter	sitter

Can You Tell?

When do the robins first chirp and
    sing,
Winter, summer, fall, or spring?

When is it hotter than spring or
    fall—
When the sun shines longer and the
    grass gets tall?

When do oak leaves become deep
    red,
And blossoms die in the flower bed?

When can the skaters glide fast on
    the lakes,
And hunters track deer in the soft
    snowflakes?

ir

| sir | fir | first | dirt |
| girl | chirp | third | birth |

or

word	work	worth	world
sailor	tailor	doctor	actor
color	favor	flavor	harbor

ur

fur	purr	burn	turn
turnip	curb	curl	hurt
turtle	nurse	purse	surprise

ar

| dollar | collar | beggar | caterpillar |
| wizard | lizard | forward | backward |

Victor and Tito

It was hot on Main Street. Victor and his cat Tito were going to the park. Tito liked to tag along at Victor's feet. Tito's fur was soft and his purr was like a deep hum. Victor liked having Tito along.

Crowds of people were on the street. Victor and Tito sat on the curb. They watched the people coming and going along the street.

A sailor went past dressed in white shirt and pants.

"I want to be a sailor," Victor said to Tito. "I want to stand on a ship and watch the color of the waves. I want to watch the sea gulls, too. I want to see the world! You can be with me, Tito. You can have fresh fish to eat."

Tito liked the flavor of fresh fish. He purred and rubbed Victor's arm.

An actor went past Victor and Tito. He had on a shining silver cape and a black top hat.

"I want to be an actor," said Victor. "I want to make the crowds cheer and clap. I want to act the part of an explorer in the jungle. You can go with me, Tito. You can be a tiger or a lion with sharp claws."

Tito purred and it was almost like the roar of a little lion.

A doctor went past on Main Street. Her eyes were kind. The doctor was smiling. Victor smiled at the doctor.

"I want to be a doctor," he said to Tito. "I want to visit people that are hurt. I want to help sick people get well. You can help me make them feel better."

Tito liked the doctor's kind eyes. Tito purred and rubbed his whiskers on Victor's leg.

Then Victor stopped smiling. "I can't be a sailor or an actor or a doctor yet. I'm just a kid. I have so long to wait."

He was sad. Then he felt Tito licking his hand. Tito jumped into his lap. The cat's whiskers tickled his chin. Victor felt better.

"Come on, Tito," said Victor. "Let's run to the park. When I get older, I'll be an actor, a sailor, or a doctor. But now, I like being a kid."

−ay

may	maybe	way	say
stay	clay	play	spray
relay	away	today	yesterday
someday	birthday	holiday	hurray

−y

by	nearby	my	myself
cry	fry	dry	try
sly	sky	skydive	skyline
why	type	fly	butterfly

The Cat

I sit soft
  On a sofa fat
And lick my velvet fur.
  I curl myself
  Into a ball
    And purr.

Adele H. Seronde

By the Sea

I say
Someday
That we shall play
By the sea,
By the sand,
By the shore.

We'll stay
And play
A long, long day
By the sea,
By the sand,
By the shore.

Adele H. Seronde

58

−y

baby	tiny	lady	lazy
happy	worry	hurry	dirty
many	very	only	every
party	fifty	family	fantasy
hungry	frisky	furry	lucky

−ly

suddenly	quickly	quietly	shortly
softly	safely	really	finally

−ey

key	valley	money	monkey

The Three Billy Goats

A long time ago, there was a lad who had three goats.

All day the billy goats leaped and skipped on a rocky hill. When it became dark and chilly, the lad drove them home to the valley.

One day he went to get the goats. But the frisky billy goats leaped over a railing into a turnip patch!

"I can't get my goats," said the little lad to himself. He sat down on the rocky hillside and began to cry.

While he was sitting there, a brown rabbit came along. The rabbit asked the lad, "Why do you cry?"

"I must drive my billy goats back home," said the lad. "But they will not leave the turnip patch. That is why I cry."

"I'll try to lead them away," said the rabbit. The rabbit tried and tried but he had to give up. The billy goats stayed in the turnip patch. The little rabbit sat down on the rocky hillside next to the lad and began to cry, too.

Along came a fox. "Why do you cry?" the fox asked the rabbit.

"This lad can't get his billy goats away from that turnip patch," said the rabbit. "That is why we cry."

"Let me try," said the fox. The fox tried to lead the billy goats away from the turnip patch. Finally, he had to give up.

So the fox sat on the rocky hillside and began to cry too.

Then a donkey came along. "Why do you cry?" asked the donkey.

"The lad's billy goats will not come away from that turnip patch," said the fox. "That is why we cry."

"Watch me do it!" said the donkey.

The donkey tried and tried, but he failed also. The billy goats still did not leave the turnip patch. So the donkey sat on the rocky hillside and began to cry with the others.

After a while, a tiny bee buzzed over the hill.

"Why do you cry?" the bee asked the donkey.

"We can't make the billy goats leave the turnip patch," said the donkey. "We have tried and tried, but they will not leave. That is why we cry."

"I can do it," said the bee. "Watch me."

The animals and the lad all stopped crying. "Ha, ha, ha! How can a tiny bee do it when we can't? You are really funny!" they said.

But the tiny bee just buzzed away to the turnip patch. The bee landed on one of the billy goats and stung it on the nose. And away ran the billy goats, every one!

soft c
ce

cent	center	cell	cellar
celery	cereal	cement	celebrate
ice	mice	nice	slice
face	race	place	space
dance	fence	once	twice
spice	office	officer	sentence

ci

circus	circle	pencil	excited
exciting	decide	recipe	medicine

cy

fancy	lacy	mercy	spicy

Going Down the Street

When I'm going
on an errand
for my mother
down the street,
I wonder
where *they're* going,
all the people
that I meet.
To the office?
To the market?
To a fancy place
to eat?

I get thinking . . .
does that lady
have a baby?
Or a pet?

Aileen Fisher

66

Tracy's Ride

Tracy was sick in bed. She had a fever. Her face was hot. Her eyes were stinging and she had a sore throat. The medicine the doctor gave her had a bad flavor.

In the yard, the sun had started to go down. Tracy was able to hear kids playing and yelling. She was able to hear mothers calling the kids in for dinner.

"I'm stuck in bed and I can't play," groaned Tracy. "It's like being in a jail cell."

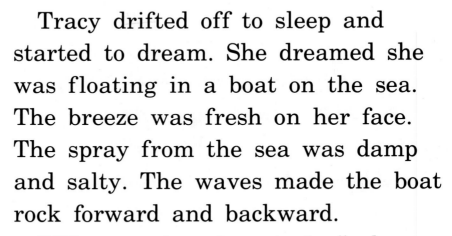

Tracy drifted off to sleep and started to dream. She dreamed she was floating in a boat on the sea. The breeze was fresh on her face. The spray from the sea was damp and salty. The waves made the boat rock forward and backward.

"What a nice place to be," she said. "It's much better than staying in bed."

Then Tracy saw whales. They made a circle. The boat was in the center. Big eyes winked up at her.

"Can I go for a ride?" she asked.

Quickly the whales swam under the little boat. Two whales lifted the boat up and raced away. Faster and faster they swam. The boat was sailing. Tracy was excited. It was almost like flying.

"Yipeeeee!" she yelled. "I'm having such fun."

Tracy woke up. It was dark. She felt her face. It was no longer hot. The nice dream had made her feel better.

"No more medicine!" she said with a big smile. "In the morning maybe Mom will let me play in the yard."

Tracy curled up under her warm blankets. She started to drift off to sleep again.

"Maybe I will have another nice . . . ."

soft g

germ	gentle	gentleman	general
giant	gigantic	giraffe	gingersnap
age	cage	page	stage
teenager	large	charge	change
strange	stranger	manage	manager
twinge	fringe	magic	tragic
damage	bandage	stingy	dingy

71

–dge

edge	ledge	hedge	pledge
ridge	bridge	badge	fudge
judge	nudge	smudge	grudge
budge	budget	dodge	lodge

The Wild Goats

The wild goats prance
    from ledge to ledge—
The wild goats dance
    to the very edge
Of the rocky ridge
    on a cliff so steep—
Which one will cross the
    sky with a leap?

Adele H. Seronde

73

Virgil's Surprise

When Virgil turned seven years old, his parents gave him a bike. He had managed to ride every day. But he only rode his bike up and down in front of his home.

Today Virgil wanted to do something more exciting.

"Dad, may I ride my bike over to Roger's?" asked Virgil. "I want to surprise him."

"Yes," said Virgil's father. "But please be careful."

Virgil had to ride up a hill to get to Roger's home. He stopped to rest when he reached the top. Virgil saw Roger's home at the bottom of a steep hill.

"Can I make it down that hill?" wondered Virgil. "Maybe I can manage if I'm very careful."

Virgil started coasting down the
hill. It was more fun coasting down
than pumping up the hill. But the
bike began to go fast. It raced along
faster and faster.

At the bottom of the hill, Virgil
lost control of the bike. He was on
the edge of the road!

Virgil slammed on his brakes.
The bike skidded. Virgil sailed over
the handlebars. He plunged into a
hedge in front of Roger's yard.

A teenager ran across the yard yelling, "Are you OK?"

"I think so," said Virgil. But when he tried to get up, he felt a twinge of pain in his ankle.

Roger came running up. "Virgil! Madge! What happened?"

"I think Virgil twisted his ankle," said Madge. "He can't get to the porch by himself. Let's help him."

"You are in luck," said Roger, "Madge's mother is a doctor. She is inside. She can fix your ankle."

"This is my mother, Dr. Lodge," said Madge.

"What happened to you?" the doctor asked Virgil.

"I fell off my bike," he said, almost in tears.

With a gentle tug, Dr. Lodge pulled off Virgil's left sneaker and sock. Then she felt his ankle and his toes. "I can't see that you did too much damage. But you have a sprained ankle. I'll put a bandage on it for you."

"My bike!" moaned Virgil. "I can't ride it home. The front wheel is bent and the back tire is flat."

Madge went over to see the damaged bike. "I think I can fix it for you," she said. "Just relax for a little while."

"I'm glad Dr. Lodge and Madge were here," said Virgil. "I told Dad I wanted to surprise you with my birthday bike. But I think the surprise was really on me."

–sion

admission   expression   mission

permission   mansion   decision

occasion   vision   television

–tion

action   nation   station

motion   lotion   education

decoration   direction   vacation

explanation   invitation   celebration

addition   position   condition

definition   attention   description

contraction   commotion   promotion

A Grand Celebration

Mr. Martinez was very excited when he came home from work. He picked up his wife and kissed her. Then he began to yell for everyone's attention.

"What's the matter?" asked his wife.

"Why are you yelling?" asked Ramón.

"Papá, what is all the commotion?" asked María.

"Come. I'll tell you," said Mr. Martinez with a big smile. "Quiet, everyone! I'll give you an explanation." He motioned for everyone to sit down.

"I had a big surprise at work today," said Mr. Martinez. "They gave me a promotion. Now my position will be manager of the entire department store."

"Hurray!" yelled María and Ramón together.

"They made a fine decision," said Mrs. Martinez. "You have worked very hard. You deserve a promotion."

"Wait!" said Mr. Martinez. "That's not all. In three weeks they are sending me to a meeting in Mexico. All of you can come along. At last we can meet the members of the Martinez family who live in Mexico."

"Bravo!" cried Mrs. Martinez and María. But Ramón was very quiet.

"Ramón, what is the matter? Why do you have such a sad expression on your face?" asked María.

"In five weeks it will be my birthday," replied Ramón. "I always have a piñata party. But this year we'll be on vacation. I'll miss my birthday party," he whined.

"But Ramón, my son, you will have an even better birthday celebration this year," said Mr. Martinez. "You can have a piñata party in Mexico!"

"Bravo!" cried Ramón. "May I invite all the Martinez family to the party?"

"Yes," replied Mrs. Martinez, "you may give everyone an invitation."

"I'm going to start packing now," said Ramón.

"Yes, you had better hurry," said Mr. Martinez, grinning at him. "After all you only have three weeks before we leave."

short oo

hood	look	took	brook
nook	shook	crook	soot
foot	football	book	bookstore
wood	wooden	wool	woolly
hook	unhook	stood	understood
cook	cookbook	good	good-bye

Come Sit With Me

Sit with me and take a look
At the pages of this book.
You won't find wizards, elves,
   or crooks,
Giant trees, or babbling brooks.
You won't find mansions made
   of wood,
Or a little girl with cape and hood;
But you'll find other things as good.
For on each page within this book
Are recipes that you can cook.

There Was a Crooked Man

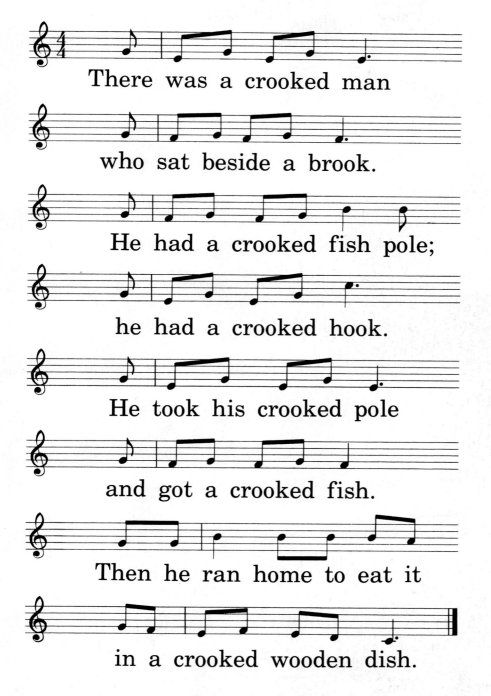

There was a crooked man

who sat beside a brook.

He had a crooked fish pole;

he had a crooked hook.

He took his crooked pole

and got a crooked fish.

Then he ran home to eat it

in a crooked wooden dish.

long oo

too	zoo	moon	noon
soon	spoon	balloon	food
cool	pool	tool	stool
proof	roof	boot	hoot
room	boom	bloom	broom
choose	loose	moose	goose
tooth	smooth	loop	stoop

Oogle Google Goblin

Hoot Tooter was a small goblin who lived in a drainpipe. The pipe was in Ronny Hooper's front yard. The pipe took away the water after a rainstorm. It was very dark and dingy down in the drainpipe.

Hoot Tooter was an oogle-google goblin. Hoot made an *oogle-google-glug-glug* whenever rain water ran down into the pipe.

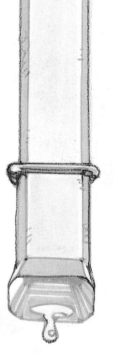

One day Ronny was playing in his yard with some string. He made a loop at the end and dropped the string into the pipe. All of a sudden, there was a big *glug*. The string jerked and shook as if there was a fish on the line.

"OOOOO . . . Oogle-google-glug! Let go of my neck!" cried someone in the pipe.

Ronny was both surprised and
scared. He pulled gently on the
string. Soon two large eyes, then a
tiny face came up over the edge of
the drainpipe. Ronny's string was
looped over the neck of a little
goblin!

"How did you get down there?"
asked Ronny.

"The Fairy Queen put me in the pipe," replied the goblin. "She is punishing me."

"What did you do?" asked Ronny.

"I scared the queen," grumbled the goblin. "I put ants on her chair. So she put me in this drainpipe and said I must stay here for a month. I have to say *oogle-google* every time water runs down the pipe."

"That's too bad," said Ronny. He was beginning to like the little goblin.

"It must be very cold and wet down there."

"It is," groaned the goblin, with a sad expression. "What's even worse, I have no one to play with."

Ronny began to feel sorry for the little goblin. He must find a way to free Hoot Tooter from that pipe.

Ronny ran up the steps. He slammed the screen door with a bang. Ronny looked in a big book for the number. Then he called the gardener who took care of his yard.

"I think the drain in my yard is stopped up," Ronny told the gardener. "It makes an *oogly-googly-glug* when water runs into it after a rainstorm. Will you please try to look at it the next time you come over?"

"I'll be glad to stop by first thing in the morning," said the gardener.

The next morning the gardener
came and looked in the drainpipe.
Then he went into action. With a
large shovel, he dug the dirt away
from the pipe. He pushed a long
wire down it. He yanked and
tugged trying to fix the pipe.

Ronny began to worry. What if
the little goblin got hurt? Ronny
watched the gardener work in his
yard all morning. When the man
finished, there was no trace of
the goblin anywhere. Ronny was
unhappy all afternoon.

That evening Ronny was almost asleep. Suddenly, the little goblin jumped onto his bed and sat down beside him.

"Thank you for getting me free from that dark, dingy drainpipe," Hoot whispered to Ronny. "When the gardener was fixing the pipe, I was able to run away."

"Did you see the queen?" asked Ronny.

"Yes, and she said I won't have to go back into the pipe. But I did have to promise never to put ants on her chair again."

"I'm glad you got away safely," said Ronny.

"Since you were so good to me," said Hoot, "I'll help you whenever you need me." Then suddenly, the little goblin was gone.

Ronny was pleased to have a goblin to help him. But he wished Hoot Tooter, the tiny goblin, was still in his front yard.

ow

owe	own	low	row
bow	bowl	mow	mower
snow	show	slow	flow
blow	blown	grow	grown
throw	thrown	yellow	fellow
pillow	hollow	follow	swallow
elbow	shadow	window	marshmallow

Little wind, blow on the hilltop,
Little wind, blow down the plain;
Little wind, blow up the sunshine,
Little wind, blow off the rain.

Kate Greenaway

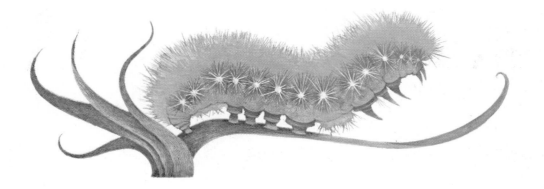

Fuzzy wuzzy, creepy crawly
Caterpillar funny,
You will be a butterfly
When the days are sunny.

Winging, flinging, dancing, springing
Butterfly so yellow,
You were once a caterpillar,
Wiggly, wiggly fellow.

Lillian Schulz Vanada

The Ant and the Grasshopper

One hot summer day, an ant was
resting in the cool shadow of a leaf.
Nearby a grasshopper was dancing
in a row of corn. He jumped and
leaped from one row to the next.
He played and sang. All summer
the grasshopper acted as if he
owned the world.

Every day the little ant saw the
grasshopper playing in the garden.
She wanted to sing and dance like
the grasshopper, but she had too much
work to do.

She picked up a grain of wheat and took it home to store for the winter. Then she went back to look for more food. It was slow and hard for her. Day after day the little ant worked to fill every room in the hollow log with good things to eat.

"Are you gathering food for winter?" the ant asked the grasshopper.

"No," replied the little fellow. "I'm having too much fun dancing and singing."

Soon winter came. Snow fell on the garden. The grasshopper was cold and hungry. He did not own a home. He did not have any food stored away for the winter.

Snow fell on the little ant's home in the hollow log. When the cold wind started to blow, she was snug and warm. She had plenty of food to eat. "Now I can sing and dance," she said, smiling to herself.

The long days had grown bitter
cold. The grasshopper was starved.
Slowly he crept to the little ant's
home. He stood up and peeked in
the window. The ant's home looked
warm and snug. Yellow drapes hung
at the window. A large bowl of food
sat on the table.

"Little Ant, Little Ant," called the
grasshopper as he scratched on the
window. "Let me in! I'm so cold and
hungry. Show me a little mercy.
Please give me a bite to eat."

"What!" cried the ant in surprise. "Don't you have any food stored away for the winter? What in the world were you doing last summer?"

"I didn't have time to store up any food," whined the grasshopper. "I was dancing and singing. Then suddenly, summer was over."

"Dancing and singing all summer, were you?" cried the ant. "Very well, now dance and sing all winter." And the little ant went back into her snug little home in the hollow log.

ou

our	sour	flour	out
about	shout	count	bounce
house	blouse	mouth	south
loud	proud	cloud	pound
compound	sound	round	around
ground	hound	found	trout

Park Play

Every morning
I can play
In the park
Across the way.

I can run
And I can shout.
I am glad
When I come out.

James S. Tippett

105

ou

four	fourth	pour	court
you	youth	soup	group
your	yours	tour	tourist
young	younger	youngster	touch
double	trouble	couple	country

All the Lassies

"I want a dog," said Peter.

"Our house is too small for a dog," replied his mother. "Besides, a dog is too much trouble."

"Just a little dog," begged Peter.

"No," said his mother, "not even a little dog. How about a fish?"

Peter named his fish Lassie. He tried to teach it to come when he called.

"Here, Lassie," he said. "Here, Lassie."

But the fish just swam round and round its bowl.

"I want a dog," Peter said.

"We don't have room for a dog," said his mother. "If you stop pestering me, I'll think about a turtle."

Peter named his turtle Lassie. He wanted it to wag its tail.

"It's not hard," he said. But the turtle looked upset. He pulled his tail into his shell. The harder Peter tried to explain, the more upset the turtle looked.

"I want a dog," he said.

"Don't you like your turtle?" his mother asked.

"I like it very much," said Peter, "but I want a dog."

"I'll speak to your father," his mother said. "Perhaps you can get a bird."

Peter named his bird Lassie. He wanted to teach her how to bark.

"Woof," he said to her very loudly. "Woof, woof, woof."

And the bird chirped back at him.

"No, Lassie," he said. "Not tweet, tweet. Woof, woof, woof!"

"I want a dog," said Peter.

"Your father found a nice kitten for you," said Peter's mother.

Peter named his kitten Lassie.

"I will roll a ball on the ground and you must bring it back to me," he explained. But the kitten did not bring it back. She batted it between her paws. The ball bounced and rolled around on the ground. Peter held the kitten on his lap and stroked her fur.

"You are a very nice kitten," he said, "but you make a terrible dog."

Peter's mother tucked him in.

"I want a dog," he said. His
mother sat on the edge of the bed.
She held his hand.

"Well," she said quietly, "perhaps
a very small dog."

They came home from the pet
shop with a large, woolly dog.

The dog came when he was
called, he wagged his tail, he had a
loud bark, and he fetched balls.

Peter named him Walter. And
Walter made very good friends with
the four Lassies.

u

utensil	usual	uniform	unite
music	museum	bugle	super

u__e

use	cube	tube	tune
prune	cute	flute	rude
rule	huge	perfume	costume
pure	cure	future	secure

ue

due	blue	cue	clue
flue	glue	Tuesday	true

ui

suit	fruit	juice	bruise
suitcase	fruitcake	juicy	cruise

Your Five Senses

What part of your body do you use to tell a red balloon from a blue one? a yellow suit from a striped suit? What do you use to read the words in this book? Do you use your eyes, ears, nose, tongue, or fingers?

One day, your dad tells you to close your eyes and open wide. Then he puts some kind of fruit in your mouth. How do you tell if it is sweet or sour? Do you smell it? See it? Feel it? Taste it? Hear it?

With your eyes closed, how can you tell a soft, square pillow from a hard, round rock? How can you tell something hot from something cold? Do you smell it? See it? Feel it? Taste it? Hear it?

How can you tell the sound of a car horn from the sound of someone singing a tune? Do you need your eyes, ears, nose, tongue, or fingers to tell you?

If you close your eyes, can you tell a cake baking from leaves burning? What do you use to tell perfume from paint? Do you use your eyes, ears, nose, tongue, or fingers?

Most of us have five wonderful senses. We have eyes to see, ears to hear, and a nose to smell. We have a tongue for tasting. And to help us decide how something feels, we have our sense of touch.

Sometimes we use more than one of our senses at a time. When you bounce a ball, three senses may be used. Can you name them?

Sense of touch, seeing, and hearing.

You can use your senses to make life fun and exciting every day. Think about what happened today or yesterday. What did you . . .

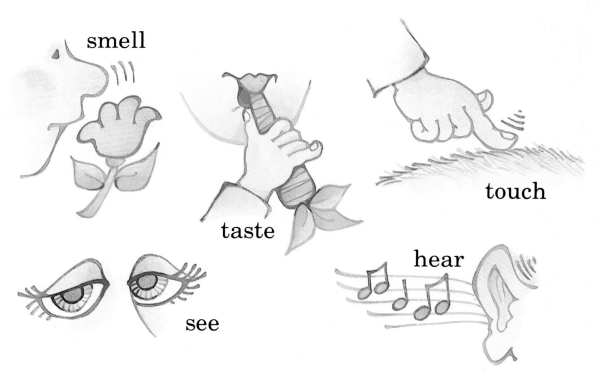

smell

taste

touch

see

hear

that helped to make it a good day?

Wild Animal Parks

In a wild animal park, animals don't live in cages. They live out in the open. People see the wild animals by driving around in the park. They must go slowly and keep the car windows rolled up.

A ranger in a striped truck watches the animals. He also watches the people. He wants to see that they follow the safety rules.

Animals that have hoofs, such as deer and elk, live well together. The big cats are kept away from them by a ditch or fence.

The Siberian tiger is the only cat that likes water.

The male lion is the only cat that has a mane around its neck.

Can you tell a tiger from a lion from a leopard?

A rhinoceros has a thick, loose hide. It looks like an animal in a suit of armor! A rhino uses the horn on its snout to defend itself. The rhino's favorite foods are grass and young, leafy branches.

An ostrich is the largest bird in the world. It probably has the longest neck, also. It cannot fly, but it can run like the wind.

Some animals come so close to
the car, you can touch them. But
don't! They may look cute or furry,
but they are still wild animals.

If you are lucky, a monkey or
a baboon may come and sit on
your car. Or a curious ostrich may
peek in the window at you. If you
are unlucky, you may get into a
traffic jam.

A giraffe is the tallest animal in the world. Giraffes have trouble eating food on the ground. In this park, food for them is placed in a tall hut. Giraffes get along well with other hoofed animals. They come and eat food the giraffes drop on the ground.

There are so many exciting things to see in a wild animal park. It's almost like being in Africa!

PHONICS CHART
Sound/Symbol Relationship Sequence

Starting Out, A

/a/aA (ant)
/n/nN (nest)
/r/rR (run)
/d/dD (dog)
/u/uU (up)
/m/mM (map)

/p/pP (pin)
/i/iI (in)
/s/sS (sun)
/o/oO (on)
/t/tT (ten)
/e/eE (egg)

/g/gG (game)
/k/cC (can)
/h/hH (hat)
/f/fF (fan)

Exploring, B

ar (art)
−er (farmer, runner)
−ed (ended, farmed,
    dropped)
/w/wW (win, warm,
    swan)
aw (saw)
ow (cow)
/l/lL, ll (let, all)

/b/bB (bed)
−le (apple)
/k/kK (kitten)
/k/ck (sack)
nk (bank)
/ā/a_e (made)
are (care)
/ē/e, ee (we, see)
/ē/ea (eat)

/ā/ai (rain)
/ī/i, i_e, ie (find,
    nine, pie)
ir (bird)
/ō/o, o_e (go, note)
or, ore (for, more)
/ō/oa, oe (coat, toe)
/j/jJ (jam)
/v/vV (vote)

Reaching Higher, C

sh (she)
ch, −tch (chin, catch)
th (then)
wh (what)
qu (queen)
xX (box)
yY (yes)
zZ (zip)
−ng (song)
−ing (jumping, sailing,
    winning, smiling)

−ed (handed, needed,
    stopped, waved)
−er (other, longer,
    baker, swimmer)
ir, ar, or, ur (girl,
    dollar, work, fur)
/ā/−ay (day)
/ī/−y (my)
/ē/−y, −ey, (happy, key)
/lē/−ly (safely)
soft c (cent, circus,
    fancy)

soft g (germ, giant,
    stingy)
−dge (edge)
−sion, −tion (admission,
    decision, motion)
short oo (book)
long oo (moon)
ow (slow)
ou (out, four, soup,
    your, young)
u, u_e (music, rule)
ue, ui (blue, suit)

continued on next page

Jumping Up, D

Formal review of
sound/symbols in
Texts, A,B,C
oi, oy (oil, boy)

ew, eau (few, beauty)
aw, au (saw, pause)
ph (photo)
gh (laugh)

ch (echo, machine)
silent w (write)
silent k (knit)

Rolling Along, E

silent b, l (comb,
talk)
silent g, h, gh (sign,
hour, right)
ea (head, great)
ear (earn, bear,
heart)

/ē/ie, ei (field, ceiling)
/ā/ei, eigh, ey (vein,
eight, they)
ough (rough, cough,
bought, though,
bough, through)
/i/y (myth)

/ī/uy, ui (buy, guide)
/i/ui (build)
/ə/ai (captain)
/e/ue (guess)
/əl/ile (missile)
silent t (listen)
silent n (autumn)